TOTALLY BRiLLiANT
COOL
PUZZLE
BOOK

ARCTURUS

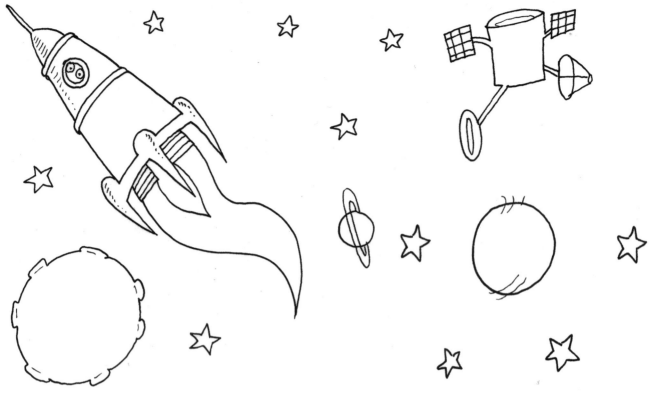

ARCTURUS

This edition published in 2015 by Arcturus Publishing Limited
26/27 Bickels Yard, 151–153 Bermondsey Street,
London SE1 3HA

ISBN: 978-1-78212-517-4
CH004027NT

Author: Lisa Regan
Illustrator: Beccy Blake
Editors: Kate Overy & Joe Fullman
Designer: Trudi Webb

Supplier 03, Date 0115, Print run 3992

Printed in China

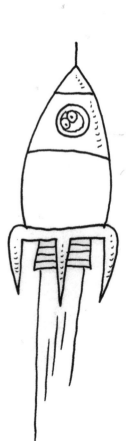

DINOSAUR BONES

Use the letters on the dinosaur ribs to find the name of the creature the dinosaur hunters have discovered.

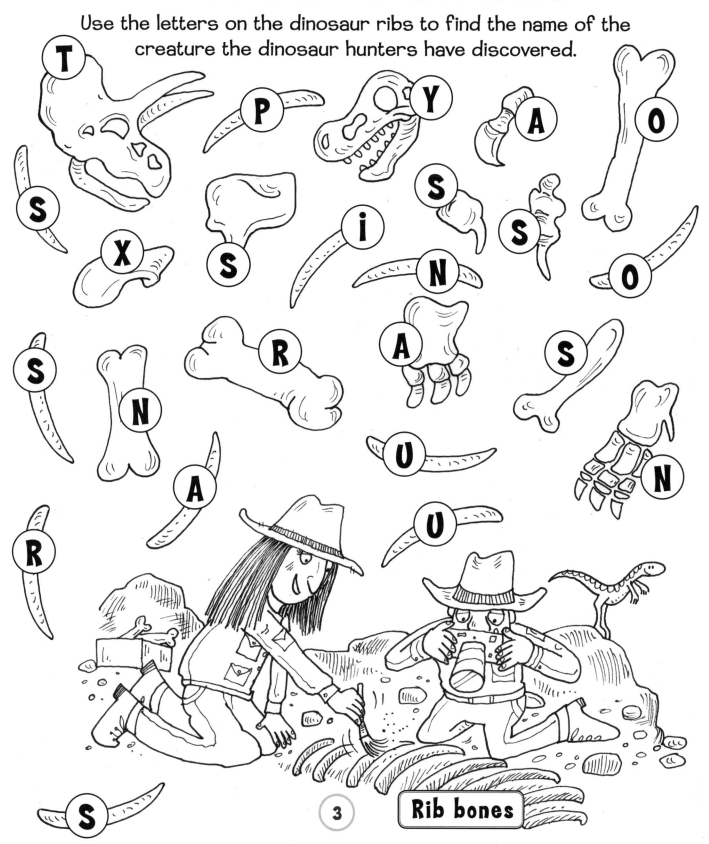

Rib bones

FORTY WINKS

Pirate Paddy is having a nap. Only one of the silhouettes matches the main picture - see if you can find the correct one.

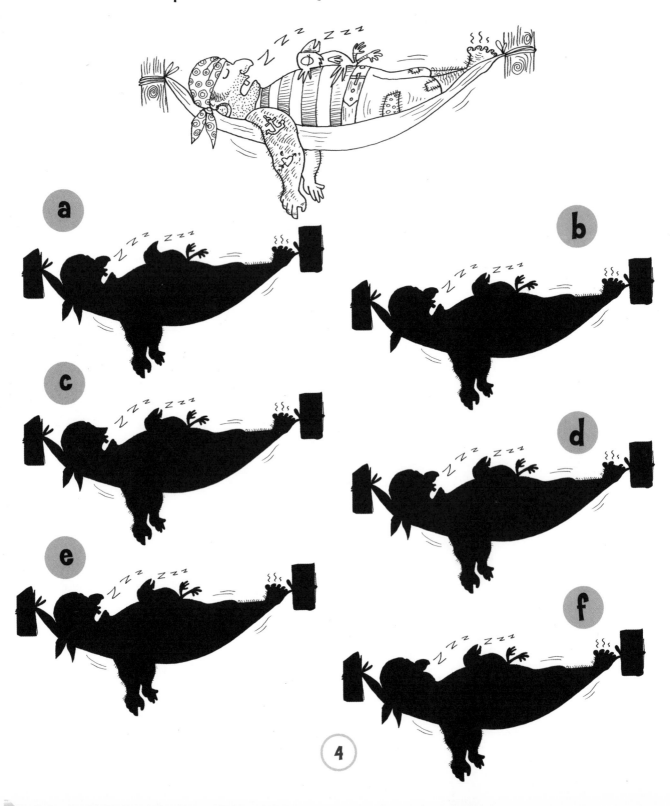

PARADISE GARDENS

Find a way through the gardens to reach the beautiful peacock!

CATWALK CREATIONS

Channel your inner fashion designer and draw your
new collection on the catwalk.

6

BLAST OFF

Search in the grid to find all of the spacecraft from the list.
They can appear across, up and down, or diagonally.

Z	V	O	Y	V	I	K	I	N	G	O	V
R	E	M	A	Y	U	Z	P	A	L	L	O
A	P	O	L	P	U	V	L	L	S	Z	Y
S	A	I	G	Y	S	V	O	S	P	R	A
P	T	N	O	G	E	P	L	Y	U	E	G
U	H	S	I	N	A	X	O	C	T	R	E
K	F	E	P	K	E	V	R	M	N	O	R
O	I	X	L	U	G	E	I	E	I	L	U
T	N	V	O	Y	M	A	R	R	K	P	A
S	D	L	P	X	E	A	L	C	S	X	S
O	E	M	A	R	I	N	E	R	M	E	G
V	R	B	T	G	E	M	I	N	I	A	A
M	A	R	Y	U	Z	O	E	N	I	K	R

VOYAGER
PIONEER
VOSTOK
MERCURY
SOYUZ
GEMINI

APOLLO
EXPLORER
SPUTNIK
MARINER
PATHFINDER
VIKING

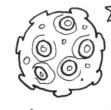

UNDER ORDERS

Agent Getya has just received her next set of instructions. Knowing that A = 3 and T = 22, can you work out what she must do next?

5.3.22.5.10

22.10.7

15.11.6.16.11.9.10.22

22.20.3.11.16   22.17

15.11.14.3.16

AMAZON ADVENTURE

There are ten differences for you to spot between these two pictures of the mighty Amazon rainforest.

OLDER AND WISER

Do the sums to work out which of the elephants is the oldest.

a) 23 + 39

b) 180 ÷ 5

c) 7 x 8

d) 18 x 3

e) 63 – 15

f) 165 ÷ 3

g) 9 x 5

CAPTAIN'S CALL

What is the Captain shouting to his crew? Use the clock code to find out.
Read the letters from each time, for example five to two spells LAZY.

Quarter to seven _ _ _ _ _

Twelve o'clock _ _

Ten to four _ _ _ _ _

Quarter past six _ _ _ _ _

Twenty five past eight _ _ _ _ _

PREHISTORIC PUZZLER

There are five things wrong with this prehistoric scene. What are they?

EAR WE GO

Match up the earrings into pairs. How many of them are left over?

WRITTEN IN THE STARS

Unscramble the letters in each group, and then work out which two labels are in the wrong place.

SPY SKILLS

Use your super spy skills to spot which two members
of this gang are the identical McDuffy twins.

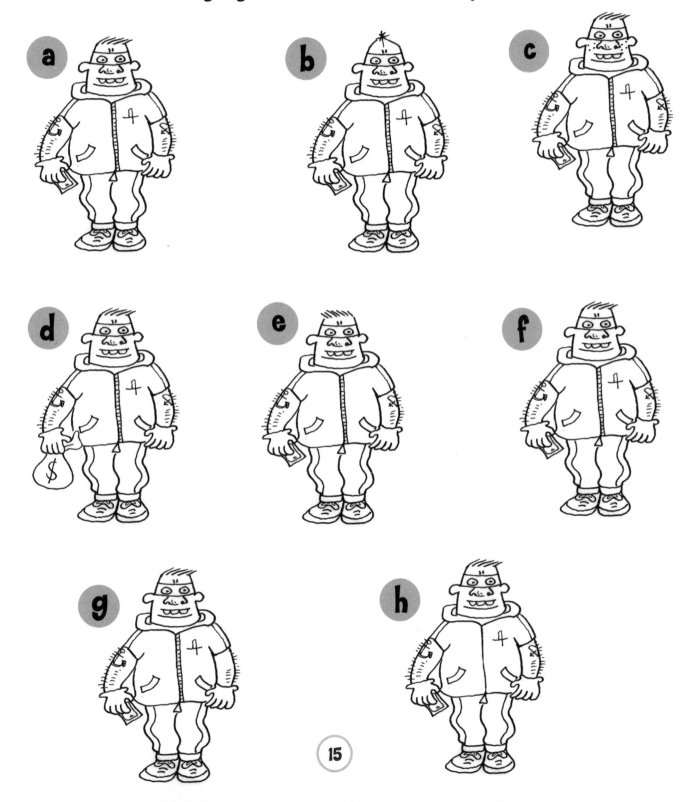

ARCHITECT'S DELIGHT

What kind of building should go here? Will it be a grand palace, a modern skyscraper, or a majestic old hall? You decide!

TURN AROUND

Make the middle fish swim in the opposite direction
by moving three of the sticks.

PRETTY POLLY

Captain Schnurrbart has lost his beloved parrot. Look for the word PARROT hidden just once in the grid.

R	A	T	T	A	R	P	A	T
P	A	R	T	P	A	O	R	P
O	T	P	A	R	A	T	T	A
R	P	R	O	T	P	A	R	R
T	O	T	O	P	A	T	A	O
A	T	O	R	R	A	P	A	O
R	P	O	R	R	A	T	P	T
R	O	T	O	P	A	R	T	O
A	O	P	A	T	O	R	A	P

STEP BACK IN TIME

Take a good look at this prehistoric scene and tick each of the circled items as you spot it.

ACCE$$ORIE$

It's time to spend some pocket money!
Work out the shopping bill for each of the girls.

OUT OF THIS WORLD

Use the grid lines to help you copy these cute aliens.
What patterns will they have?

TOP SECRET

How many words containing three or more letters can you make from the phrase below? One has been done to get you started.

FOR YOUR EYES ONLY

1. NOSE
2. _____
3. _____
4. _____
5. _____
6. _____
7. _____
8. _____
9. _____
10. _____
11. _____
12. _____
13. _____
14. _____
15. _____
16. _____

DREAM DESTINATION

Fill in the grid so that each row, column, and minigrid contains the numbers 1 to 6. The number that doesn't feature in the shaded squares is the next place Ayesha wants to visit.

MAN'S BEST FRIEND

Which of the dogs has Ritchie decided to adopt from the Rescue home? Use the clues to work it out.

It doesn't have a collar on.

Its ears aren't long and droopy.

Its tail is fluffy.

It doesn't have a patch over its eye.

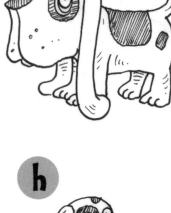

UNDER FIRE

Help Pirate Patrick back to his ship,
dodging the cannonballs along the way.

LOOK OUT!

Only one of the silhouettes matches the main picture
- see if you can find the correct one.

a

b

c

d

e

f

COVER UP

Beccy can't decide which jacket to wear. Shade in any letter that appears more than once to find out which one she chooses.

D	N	B	i
W	L	M	A
i	Z	D	N
E	M	W	R

INTO SPACE

What kind of spacecraft would you like to travel in?
Design your own here, ready for liftoff.

FOREIGN EXCHANGE

A good spy needs to know all about the countries they are posted to.
Find each of these currencies in the grid; you never know
when you might need some local money!

RUBLE	FRANC	EURO
RUPEE	YUAN	DINAR
DOLLAR	PESO	YEN
DIRHAM	REAL	FORINT

D	i	R	U	B	Y	U	A	N	F
R	U	B	L	E	E	O	D	i	O
F	D	O	L	V	R	i	i	F	R
R	i	L	R	R	U	D	N	O	i
A	D	O	Y	E	U	R	A	R	N
N	O	i	E	U	P	P	R	E	T
C	L	O	R	E	D	R	E	A	D
N	L	F	S	H	O	i	Y	E	N
i	A	O	R	F	A	N	E	i	E
D	R	R	E	A	L	M	D	E	P

WHAT ON EARTH?

If A = Z and B = Y, what on earth does this message say?

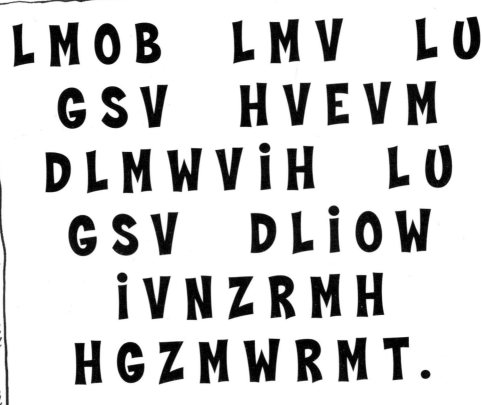

LMOB LMV LU
GSV HVEVM
DLMWVIH LU
GSV DLIOW
IVNZRMH
HGZMWRMT.

BIRDS OF A FEATHER

There are ten differences for you to spot between these two beautiful bird pictures.

READY FOR BATTLE

Work out which letters are missing from the alphabet here, and then rearrange them to find which body part these dinosaurs had in common.

A G B H R
V X C N O Y
Z D F T J
L W M

IT MUST BE GLOVE

How many gloves are there in this store?

SKY MAP

Find a way from the top to the bottom of the grid,
following the symbols in this order: 🪐 ☆ ☾

DECODED

A 'birdwatcher' is a nickname for a spy.
Which set of letters cannot be unscrambled
to spell the word correctly?

DITCHWARBER

CHERARWATBE

BADRICHERWT

CHEATDRIWBR

ITCHWARDBER

HERDCATBIWR

GOING STRAIGHT

Sneaky Luigi has been selling fake souvenirs at the Leaning Tower of Pisa, but now he wants to clean up his act. Which of the models is the odd one out, to be thrown away?

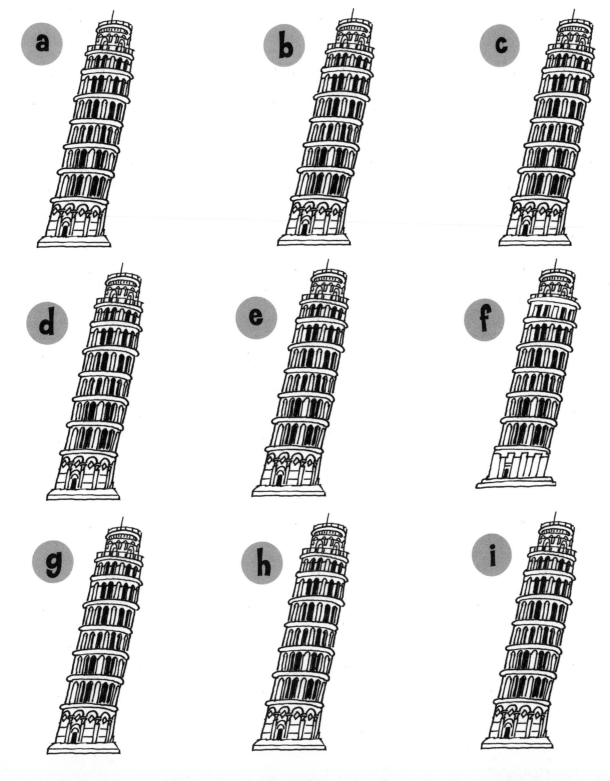

AS TALL AS...

Everyone knows that the giraffe is the tallest animal in the world. But what exactly is this one as tall as? Draw something for comparison - sensible or silly!

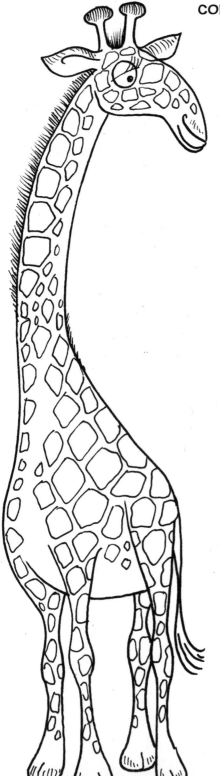

DUPED!

The ship's cook is always conning poor Chico the cabin boy out of his wages. Help Chico to figure out this puzzle and keep his coins.

Take away six coins so that each row and column has an even number of coins left.

Clue: One row and one column still have four coins in.

DEM BONES

How many times can you find the word BONE hidden in this dinosaur dig?

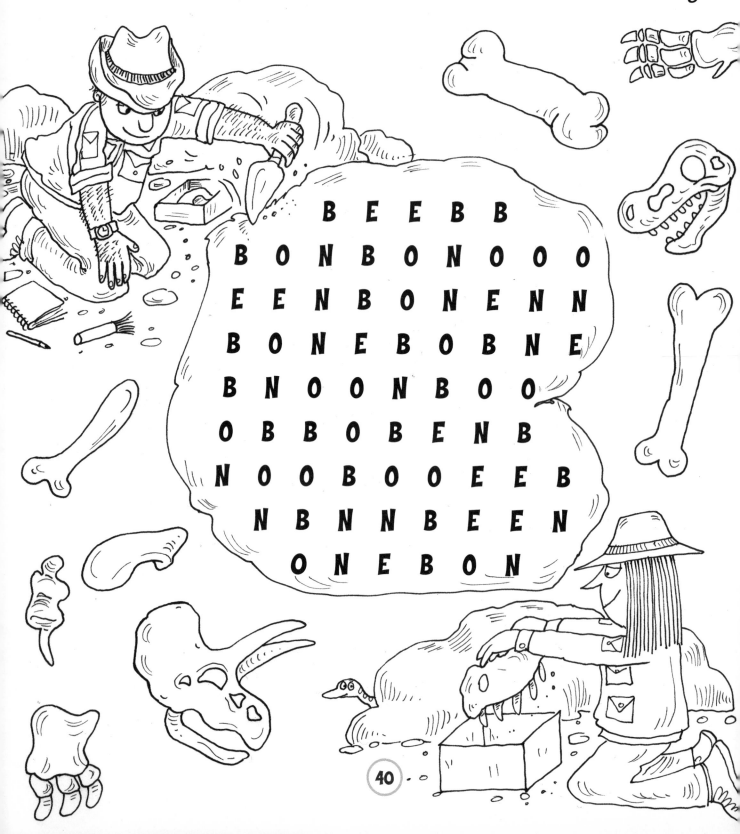

B E E B B
B O N B O N O O O
O E E N B O N E N N
B O N E B O B N E
B N O O N B O O
O B B O B E N B
N O O B O O E E B
E N B N N B E E N
O N E B O N

CATWALK CRAZY

Check out this fashion parade and tick each of
the circled items as you spot it.

BRAIN TEST

Which two switches does the astronaut need to flick to make them point to numbers that add up to 100?

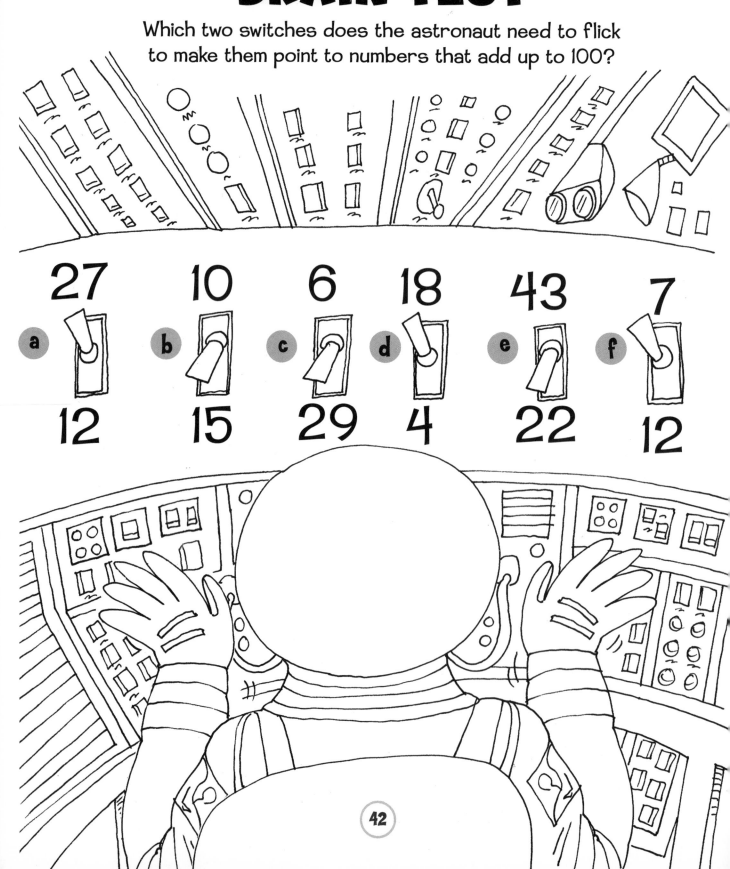

27   10   6   18   43   7

a   b   c   d   e   f

12   15   29   4   22   12

ON THE PROWL

Our spies have tracked down one of the bad guys!
Can you copy his picture, using the grid, to circulate his ID?

ANCIENT WONDER

How many words containing three or more letters can you make from the phrase below? One has been done to get you started.

HANGING GARDENS

1. GRAND
2. _____
3. _____
4. _____
5. _____
6. _____
7. _____
8. _____
9. _____
10. _____
11. _____
12. _____
13. _____
14. _____
15. _____
16. _____

MOO-DOKU

Fill in the grid so that each row, column, and minigrid contains each of the animal sounds.

SQUEAK					BAA
	ROAR		MOO		SQUEAK
MOO			WOOF		
	BAA	WOOF		MOO	
	WOOF	SQUEAK		ROAR	
ROAR		NEIGH			WOOF

SAILING THE SEAS

Use the clues to work out where each pirate is going to, and which animal he keeps as a pet.

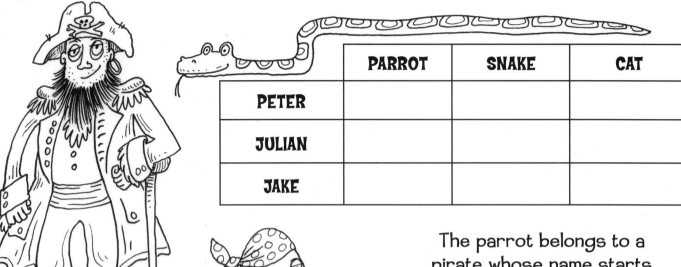

	PARROT	SNAKE	CAT
PETER			
JULIAN			
JAKE			

The parrot belongs to a pirate whose name starts with J.

Jake is not sailing to an island.

The owner of the cat is going to Jamaica.

The pirate bound for Puerto Rico owns a parrot.

	JAMAICA	CHINA	PUERTO RICO
PETER			
JULIAN			
JAKE			

FANCY FLIER

Which of the exits leads to the pteranosaur in the middle of the maze?

MYSTERY MANNEQUIN

Which of the shadows has been cast by the dummy
in the middle of the shop?

FAR FLUNG

Cross out any letters that appear two or more times. The remaining letters will spell the destination for your next space mission.

M V T J E

P J N P

T

A U A

M S

49

UNDER COVER

A spy should be a master of disguise. Help these agents change their faces so that even their own parents wouldn't know them!

TOP OF THE WORLD

Listed below are some of the planet's greatest waterfalls, volcanoes and mountains. Find them all hidden in the grid.

NIAGARA

TUGELA

ANGEL

VICTORIA

VESUVIUS

KILIMANJARO

ELBRUS

MAUNA KEA

EVEREST

LOGAN

ACONCAGUA

MCKINLEY

L	M	A	U	N	T	V	N	I	A	Y	M
A	O	V	M	A	U	N	A	K	E	A	A
A	C	G	I	C	G	A	M	L	V	T	N
C	I	O	A	E	I	N	N	C	U	V	I
O	V	N	N	N	V	I	C	G	K	E	A
N	A	I	G	K	K	E	I	L	E	V	V
C	C	A	C	C	I	K	R	L	V	L	E
A	N	G	M	T	U	G	B	E	C	V	S
G	I	A	I	U	O	R	L	N	S	I	U
U	A	R	N	G	U	R	E	G	V	T	V
A	N	A	V	S	N	V	I	A	M	A	I
K	I	L	I	M	A	N	J	A	R	O	U
B	M	C	K	T	U	G	E	L	A	R	S

ZOO TRIP

Decode the animal signs and fill in the key below (don't worry, you won't be able to fill in all the letters). Then work out what the oval signs say.

READY, AIM, FIRE!

Watch out! These pirates are a mean bunch.
Find ten differences between the two pictures.

OLDER THAN OLD

Solve the problem on each dinosaur (working from left to right). The one with the largest number lived the longest time ago, and the smallest answer is on the dinosaur that lived most recently.

$50 \times 6 + 40 - 20 \div 8$

$14 + 33 \times 2 + 100 - 19 \div 5$

$212 - 80 \div 6 - 7 \times 2$

DRESSING UP

Sasha has a fancy dress party to go to. Work out which letters are missing from each alphabet to find the items she needs for her costume.

NOPHIJK
MVWXQRS
UACDFGYZ

AHFVXGK
LQSTUM
IJBDEPYZ

55

WATERY WORLD

How many alien fish are there in this space scene?

56 Alien Fish ⟶

POINTING THE FINGER

Study the fingerprints carefully. Each of them has an identical match, and it's your job to pair them up.

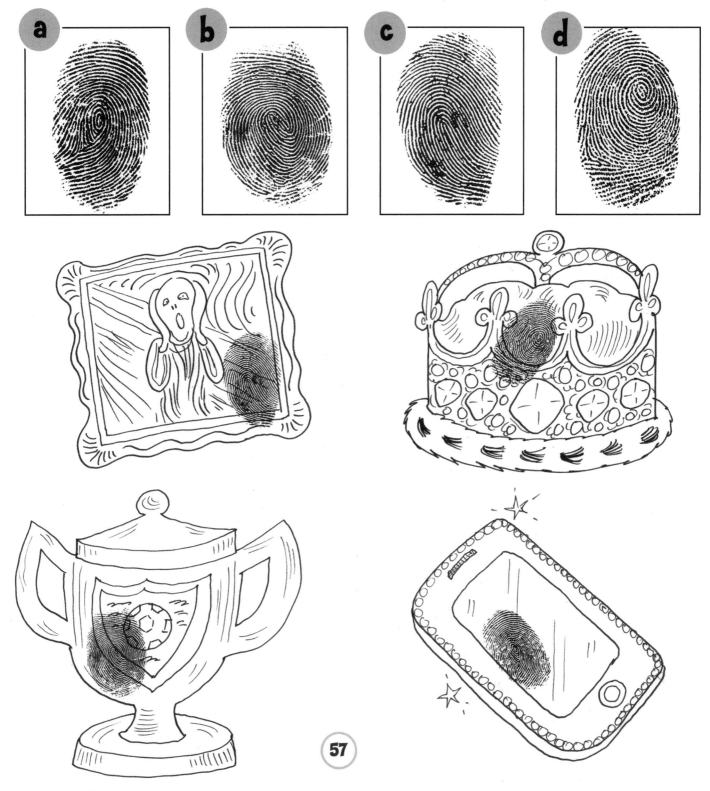

A LITTLE BIT LOST

Unscramble each set of letters to find six countries
and then relocate them to their proper continent.

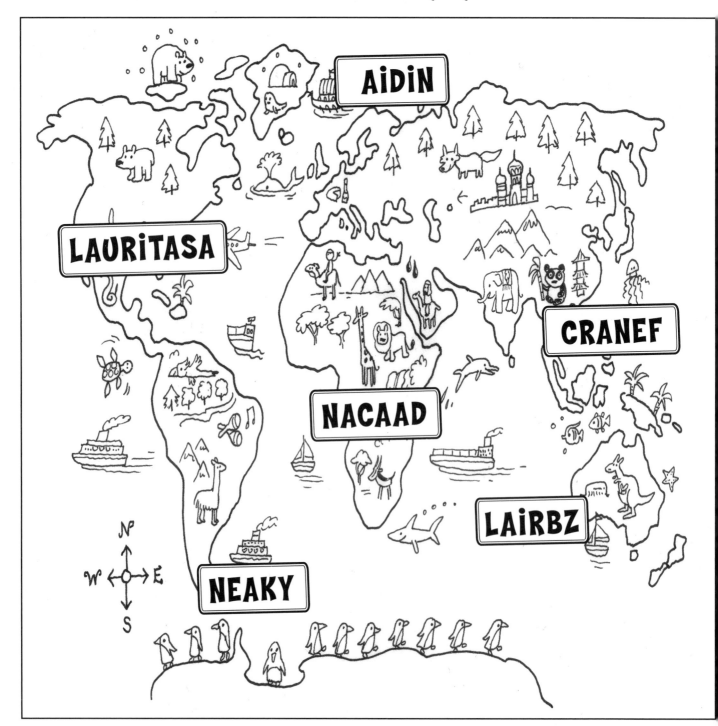

AIDIN

LAURITASA

CRANEF

NACAAD

LAIRBZ

NEAKY

PROUD AS A PEACOCK

Which two of these peacocks are exactly the same?

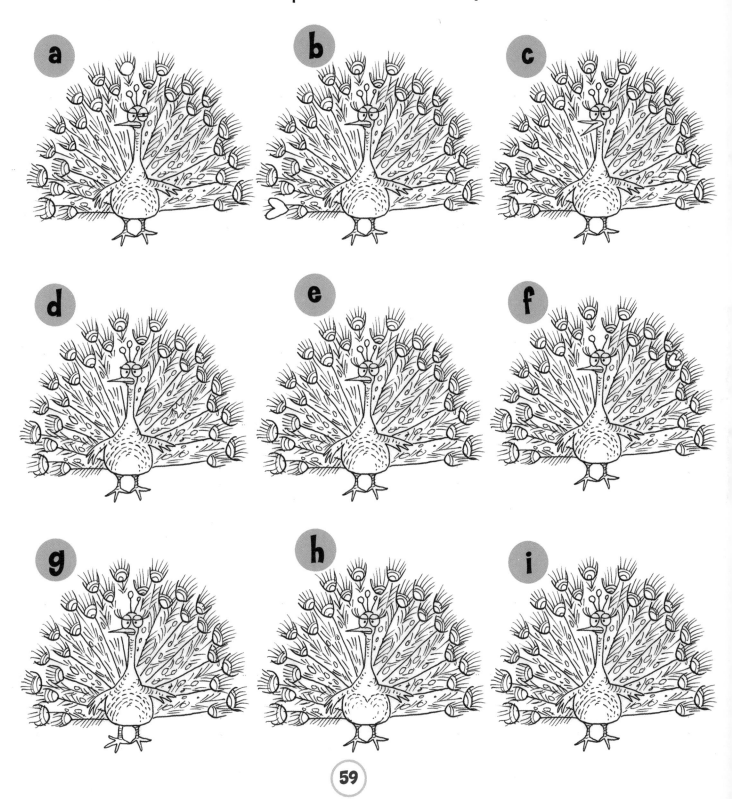

MAP MAKING

Draw your own pirate map to show where buried treasure lies. Use the items around the edge to inspire you.

TROODON AND THE TWIGS

See if you're cleverer than the so-called brainy dinosaur with this puzzle. How do you move just two sticks to make seven squares?

GIRL'S BEST FRIENDS

How many times can you find the word DIAMOND hidden in the grid?

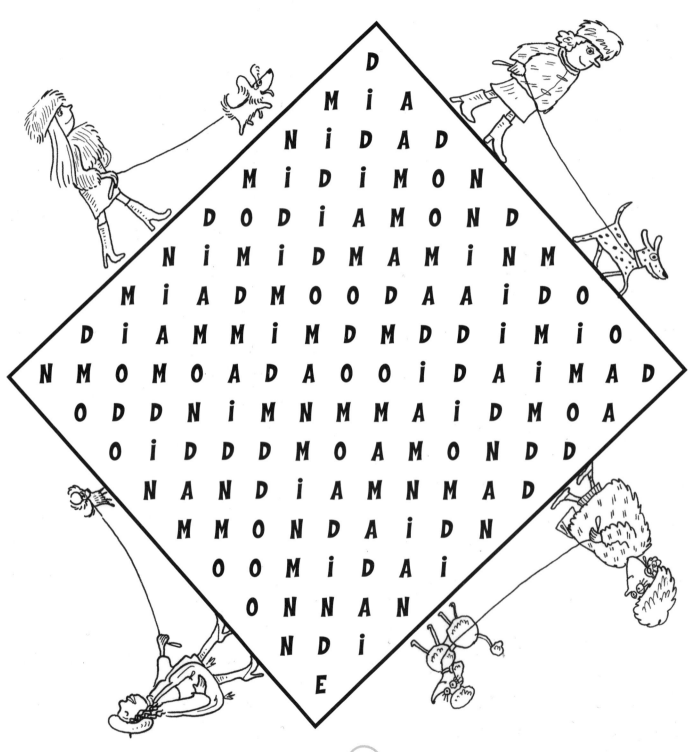

GALACTIC GOODIES

This restaurant is out of this world! Tick each
of the circled items as you find it.

HOUSE ARREST

The spies all received the same mathematical instructions for their next location. Which of them is spying on the correct house?

days in a week
+
sides on a hexagon
x
legs of a crow
−
books in the Lord of the Rings series

STANDING TALL

Use the grid lines to help you copy this picture of the Statue of Liberty.
Make sure she has seven spokes on her crown!

HOP IT!

How many words containing three or more letters can you make from the phrase below? One has been done to get you started.

RUN RABBIT RUN

1. RAIN
2. _____
3. _____
4. _____
5. _____
6. _____
7. _____
8. _____

9. _____
10. _____
11. _____
12. _____
13. _____
14. _____
15. _____
16. _____

TROPICAL TIME

Fill in the grid so that each row, column and minigrid contains the numbers 1 to 6. Which number goes inside the circle? That is the number of weeks before Pirate Jim has to head for home.

EGGS-ACTLY

Use three straight lines to divide the land into six sections, with two dinosaur eggs in each section.

SHOPPING TRIP

Help Trudi find her way back through the shopping mall to the food court in the middle.

3-2-1-LIFTOFF

Only one of the spaceship silhouettes matches the main picture - see if you can find the correct one.

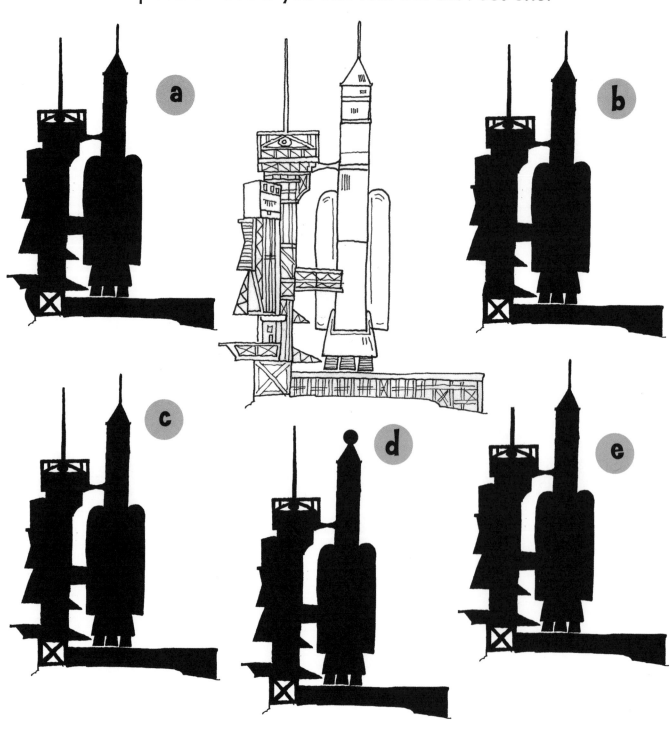

MAKE HASTE!

Cross out every other letter to reveal the hidden message.

FROM LOL
NOT WATCH
HER MY
AUNT IS NOT
SHOE UV
RAIN

WISH YOU WERE HERE

Where in the world would you most like to visit?
Design postcards from your top destinations.

Wish you were here

What an amazing view!

FEATHERED FRIENDS

Look in the grid to find each of the birds on the list;
they can appear across, up and down, or diagonally.

PENGUIN   SWAN   ROBIN
OWL   TOUCAN   CROW
HAWK   KIWI   PELICAN
CUCKOO   CANARY   RHEA

T	K	C	N	O	R	W	i	P	O
O	i	A	C	K	O	O	i	E	U
U	W	A	H	A	W	K	B	L	P
S	T	O	U	C	A	N	O	i	E
R	C	G	K	O	O	i	Y	C	N
C	O	U	R	O	W	A	R	A	G
U	P	L	C	i	A	E	A	N	U
K	W	E	K	K	H	H	N	W	i
O	P	E	L	i	O	R	A	i	N
C	R	O	W	P	E	O	C	K	R

SAY WHAT?

If A = 6 and J = 15, work out what on earth
Captain Crowface is talking about.

28.10.17.17

8.26.23.24.10   18.30

8.26.25.17.6.24.24   6.19.9

16.19.20.8.16   18.10   9.20.28.19

28.14.25.13   6   21.6.23.23.20.25

11.10.6.25.13.10.23!

74

NIGHT AT THE MUSEUM

Jumping velociraptors! Something's afoot at the museum.
Spot ten differences between the two pictures.

SAFE STASH

Work out the code to open the safe and store the tiara away safely.

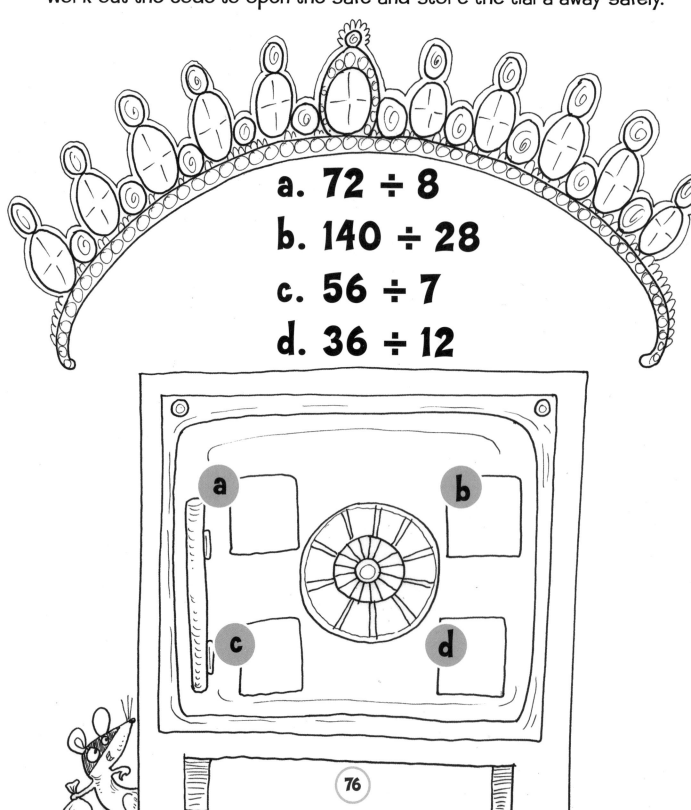

a. 72 ÷ 8

b. 140 ÷ 28

c. 56 ÷ 7

d. 36 ÷ 12

SPACE-TIME

Use the clock code to fill in the astronaut's schedule. Read the letters from each time, for example twenty five past nine spells STAR.

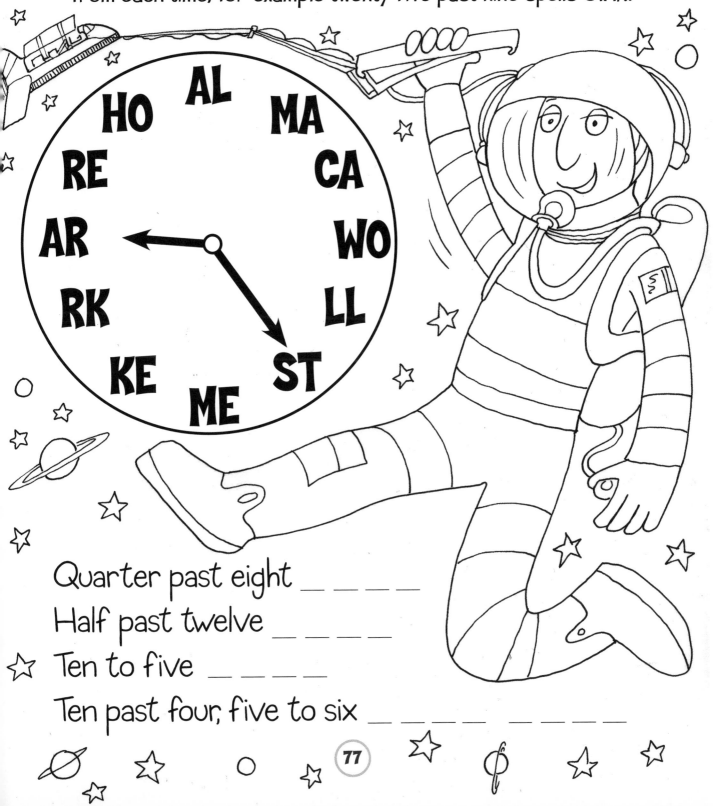

Quarter past eight _ _ _ _ _

Half past twelve _ _ _ _

Ten to five _ _ _ _ _

Ten past four, five to six _ _ _ _ _ _ _ _ _

SHALL WE DANCE?

Use your spy skills to discover how many secret 'flower' listening devices have been hidden at the grand ball.

HIT THE RIGHT NOTES

The soprano at the Sydney Opera House is in fine voice. Find a path through the music, following the notes in this order:

GOING APE

This orangutan is all in a muddle. Which is the only group of letters that spells his name properly?

ODDER AND ODDER

Which of the pirate parrots is the odd one out in this already-odd bunch?

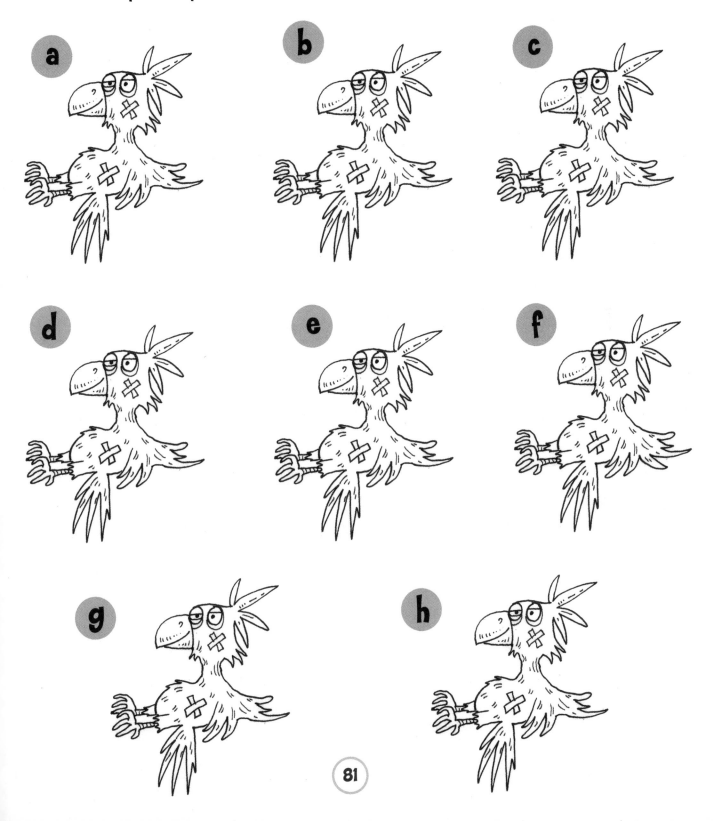

RUNNING SCARED

What is this little dinosaur running away from? You decide!

HATS OFF!

Put your thinking cap on to work out the answer to this fashion dilemma.

AMY HAS 14 HATS. ALL OF THEM ARE WHITE OR BLACK, AND SHE HAS FOUR MORE WHITE ONES THAN BLACK ONES. HOW MANY WHITE HATS DOES SHE OWN?

SEEING STARS

What has Professor Castle discovered through her telescope?
Use the grid references to work it out.

	1	2	3	4
a	D	P	N	U
b	T	L	G	R
c	O	S	E	A
d	B	i	C	M

1. d3.c1.d4.c3.b1

2. c4.c2.b1.c3.b4.c1.d2.a1

3. b4.c3.a1 / b3.d2.c4.a3.b1

4. a3.c3.d1.a4.b2.c4

84

SOMETHING SUSPICIOUS

There are four spies staking out the airport.
Use the photos to help you spot them.

TRAVEL GUIDE

Work out the price on each ticket to find out
who is visiting each of the sights.

a

$$3 \times (15 - 4) \times (12 \div 4)$$

b

$$2 \times (60 \div 3) + (3 \times 15)$$

c

$$9 \times (4 + 5) + (13 \times 3)$$

d

$$3 \times (27 \div 9) \times (75 \div 5)$$

85

120

135

99

SLEEPING LIONS

Use the grid lines to help you copy this lion. Shh!
You don't want to wake him up!

WAKEY WAKEY!

How many words containing three or more letters can you make from the phrase below? One has been done to get you started.

SHIVER ME TIMBERS

1. RESIST
2. _____
3. _____
4. _____
5. _____
6. _____
7. _____
8. _____

9. _____
10. _____
11. _____
12. _____
13. _____
14. _____
15. _____
16. _____

DINO-DOKU

Fill in the grid so that each row, column, and minigrid contains the letters A to F. The letter in the bottom left square tells you which dinosaur Danny likes the best.

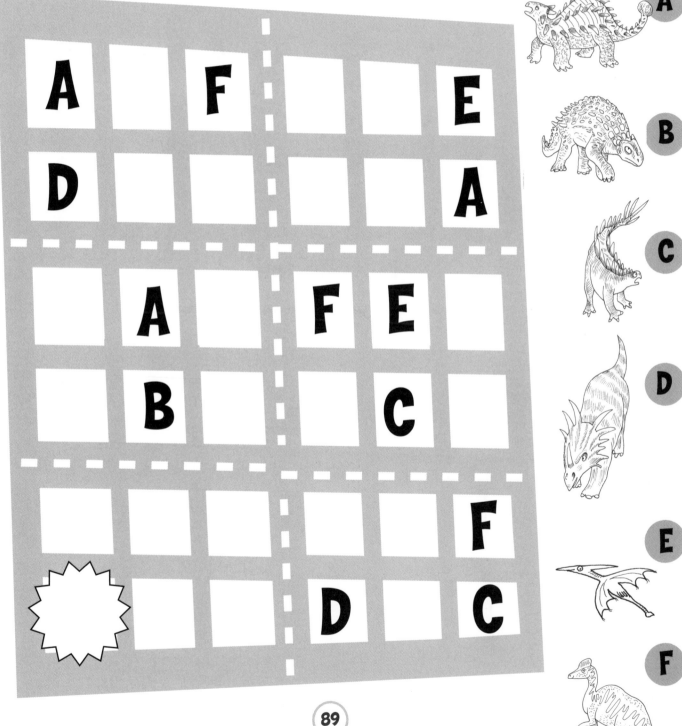

DESIGN DIVA

Use the clues to work out which of these designers is fashion guru Riccardo Gulliano.

He is wearing a hat.
He doesn't have a beard.
Today he's sporting a tie.
He has taken off his shades.

c

d

e

f

g

h

SUPERNOVA

Watch out for the exploding star! Find a way out, as fast as you can.

MRS BAD GUY

Which of these shadow outlines matches the mysterious Madame Malevio?

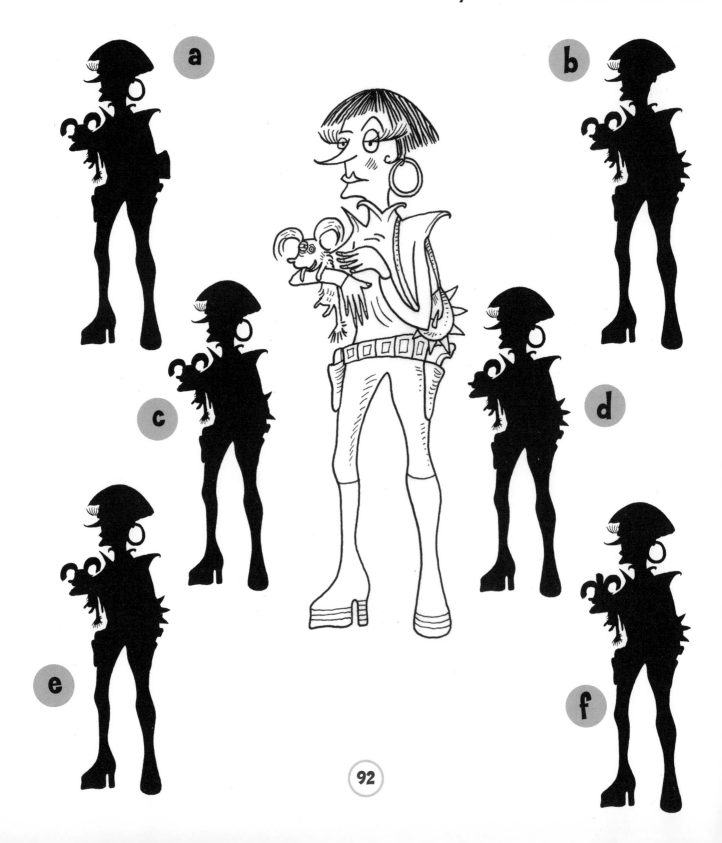

TAKE ME TO THE TEMPLE

Cross out all the letters that appear more than once to reveal the country where the ancient Temple of Artemis was built.

T N R D
U N P
A P
O
K A O
S D S
E Y

WHO NOSE?

What animal do these nose and whiskers belong to?
Draw a creature you love, or make one up!

ROLL CALL

Three of the pirates have jumped ship! Search in the grid to find all of the names, and see which three are missing.

PEDRO   **PERCY**   **PRASAD**
PABLO   **PERRY**   **PRESLEY**
PALMER   **PIERCE**   **PETER**
PARKER   **PLACIDO**   **PACO**

P	P	E	R	P	A	P	E	T	P
P	A	E	P	R	A	S	A	D	i
A	P	D	T	P	P	A	P	O	P
R	P	R	M	E	P	A	A	P	P
K	L	E	P	R	R	P	C	A	A
E	A	i	D	A	E	L	O	L	B
R	C	P	D	R	T	P	P	M	L
E	i	E	C	M	O	O	A	i	O
R	D	Y	P	i	E	R	C	E	P
P	O	P	O	P	P	R	E	S	L

DINO CODE

If A = D and L = O, can you work out what these dinosaur exhibits actually are?

VWBUDFRVDXUXV

PLQPL

WEDDING BELLES

Everyone is in their finest clothes for the wedding of the year!
Can you spot ten differences between the two wedding photos?

LET ME IN!

Unlock the hatch by entering the correct code into the controls.

a Days in a leap year ÷ 6

b Rainbow stripes x 4

c Sides on a cube + 8

ON THE RUN

Agent Getcha has been given her next destination. Work out which letters of the alphabet are missing and use them to spell a city in Europe.

MISSING THE POINT

There are five things wrong with the picture on this postcard from the Egyptian desert. What are they?

CHANGING TIMES

Each of these chameleons has a twin that looks the same - except one.
Can you find it?

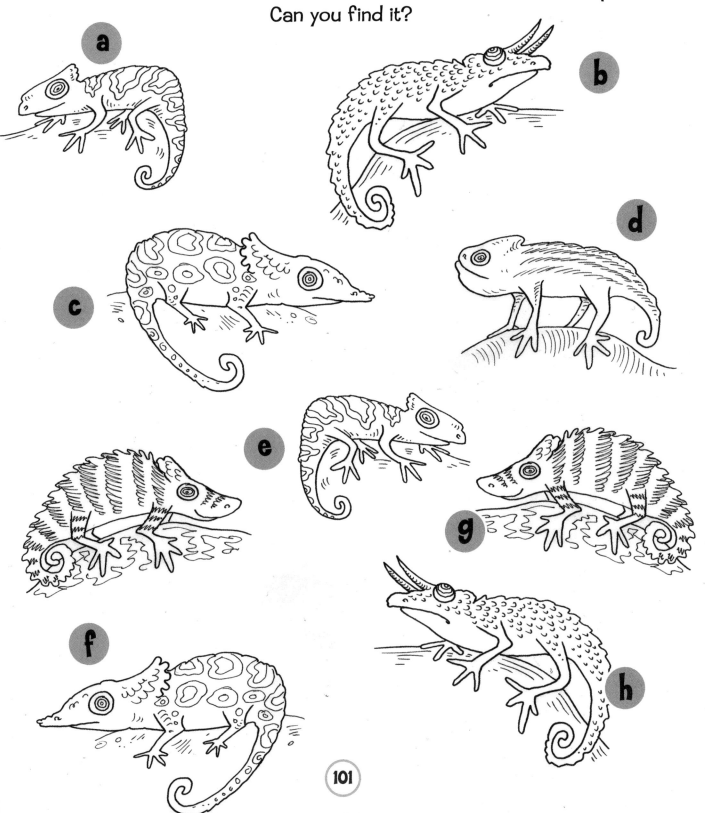

ALL AT SEA

Which of the sets of letters, when unscrambled,
does not spell BUCCANEER?

CANEBUCER

NECEBUCAR

UCCANNEBR

BUNCREECA

URBANCEEC

CRANECUBE

DUCK-BILLS

Which of these crested corythosaurus is the odd one out?

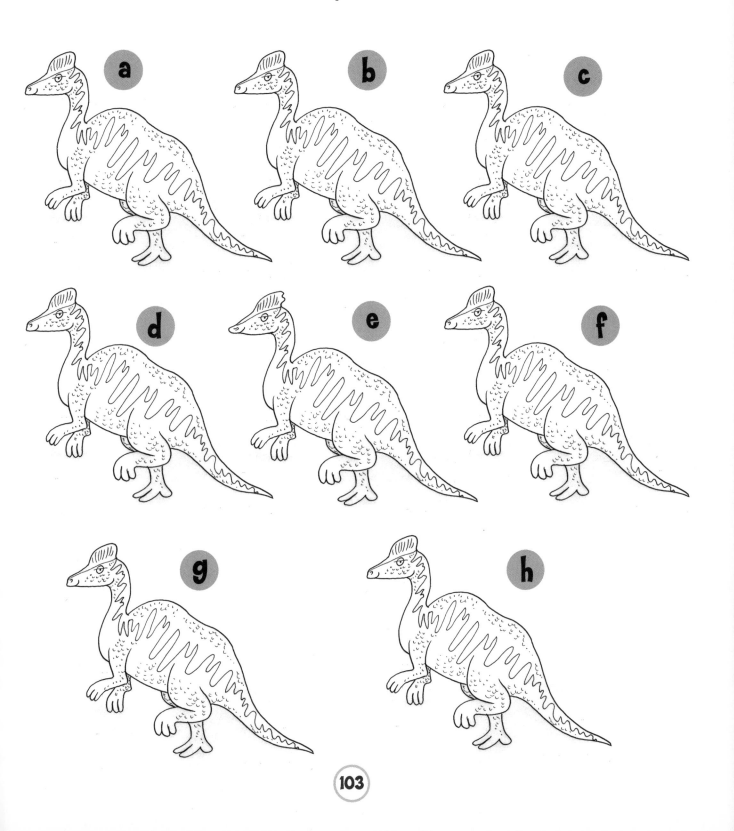

CASUAL CREATIONS

Add your own creative twist to these vests and t-shirts - dress them up with diamante or down with graffiti, to suit your mood.

SPACE DOG

Astronomers have found a new constellation, nicknamed Fido.
Some say it's facing left, others say it's facing right.

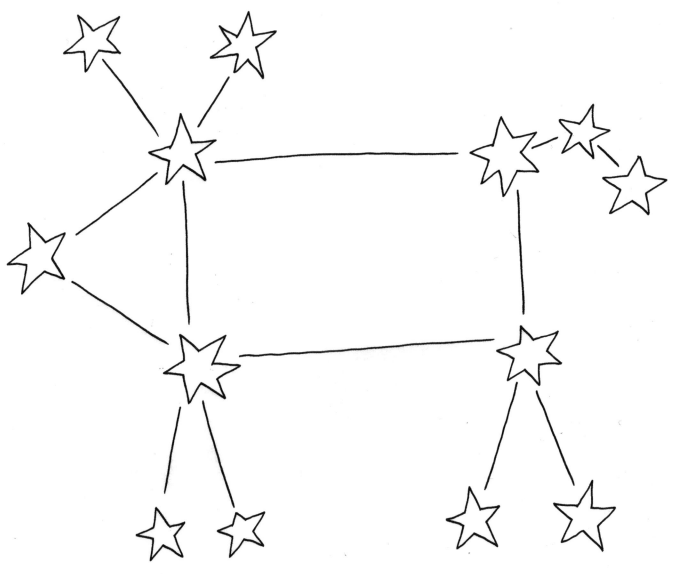

Where would you move a single star that could make it look to be facing the other way?

DOUBLE AGENT

Can you find the word AGENT hidden twice in the grid?

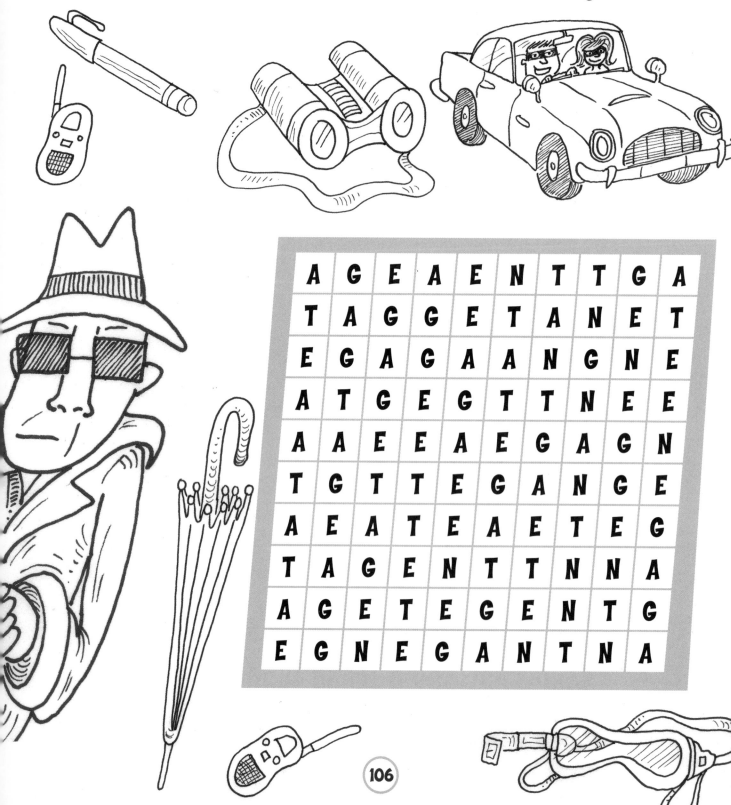

A	G	E	A	E	N	T	T	G	A
T	A	G	G	E	T	A	N	E	T
E	G	A	G	A	A	N	G	N	E
A	T	G	E	G	T	T	N	E	E
A	A	E	E	A	E	G	A	G	N
T	G	T	T	E	G	A	N	G	E
A	E	A	T	E	A	E	T	E	G
T	A	G	E	N	T	T	N	N	A
A	G	E	T	E	G	E	N	T	G
E	G	N	E	G	A	N	T	N	A

WONDERS OF THE SEA

Take a good look around the Great Barrier Reef
and tick each of the circled items as you spot it.

PET PRESENTS

Danny wants to buy a dog toy for his beloved pet, Buster.
See if you can work out how much money he needs.

These three toys cost 5.50.

These three toys cost 6.00.

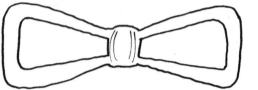 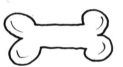

These three toys cost 5.00.

 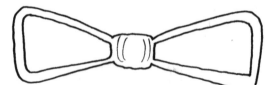

How much does a bone on its own cost?

AYE AYE, CAP'N

Use the grid lines to help you copy the pirate captain. Aharrrgh!

RUN AWAY!

How many words containing three or more letters can you make from the phrase below? One has been done to get you started.

TYRANNOSAURUS REX

1. ROARS
2. _____
3. _____
4. _____
5. _____
6. _____
7. _____
8. _____
9. _____
10. _____
11. _____
12. _____

13. _____
14. _____
15. _____
16. _____
17. _____

GEM-DOKU

Fill in the grid so that each row, column, and minigrid contains each type of glittering earring.

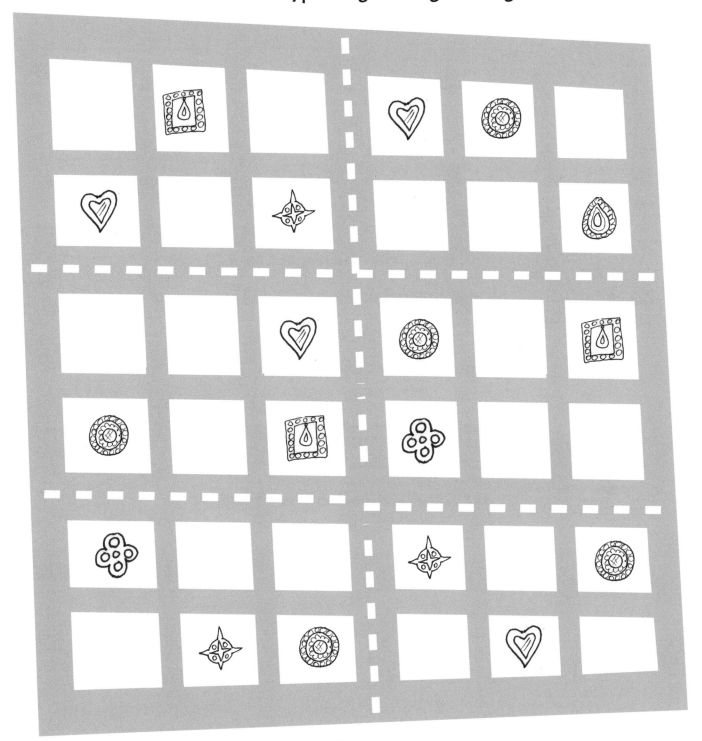

ALIEN WORKOUT

Use the clues to fill in the grid and work out what each alien is called, and where it calls home.

1

	PIFF	PAFF	BURP
1			
2			
3			

Piff is not from the planet Snark.

The alien from Jootle has two eyes.

Paff has no tail.

Creatures from Bilge have an odd number of eyes.

The alien from Snark has the longest neck.

The creature with big teeth is not Piff.

The name of the alien from planet Jootle begins with P.

2

3

	SNARK	JOOTLE	BILGE
1			
2			
3			

HUNT HIM DOWN

START

Help undercover agent Jim track down the counterfeiter
by working your way through the maze.

FINISH

AMAZING ATOMIUM

Study the silhouettes of the fantastic Atomium in Belgium and see which one of them matches the picture exactly.

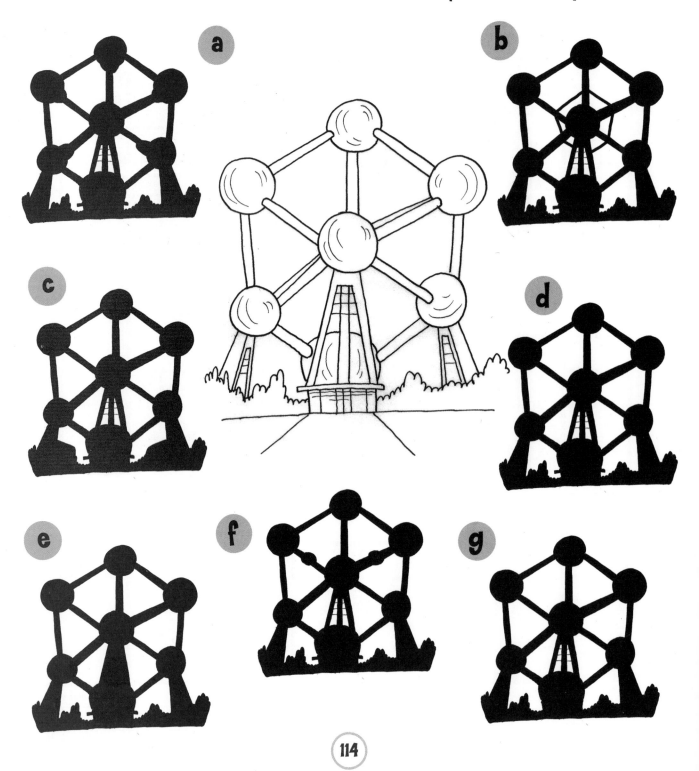

ON THE MOVE

Use the letters on the snails that are heading left to find out what type of creature snails are.

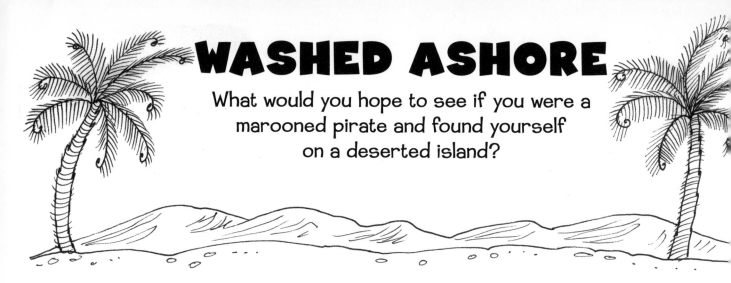

WASHED ASHORE

What would you hope to see if you were a
marooned pirate and found yourself
on a deserted island?

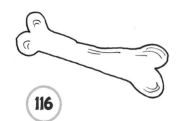

ALL FOR ONE

This Stegosaurus looks alarmed!
Can you find a single ALLOSAURUS hiding in the grid?

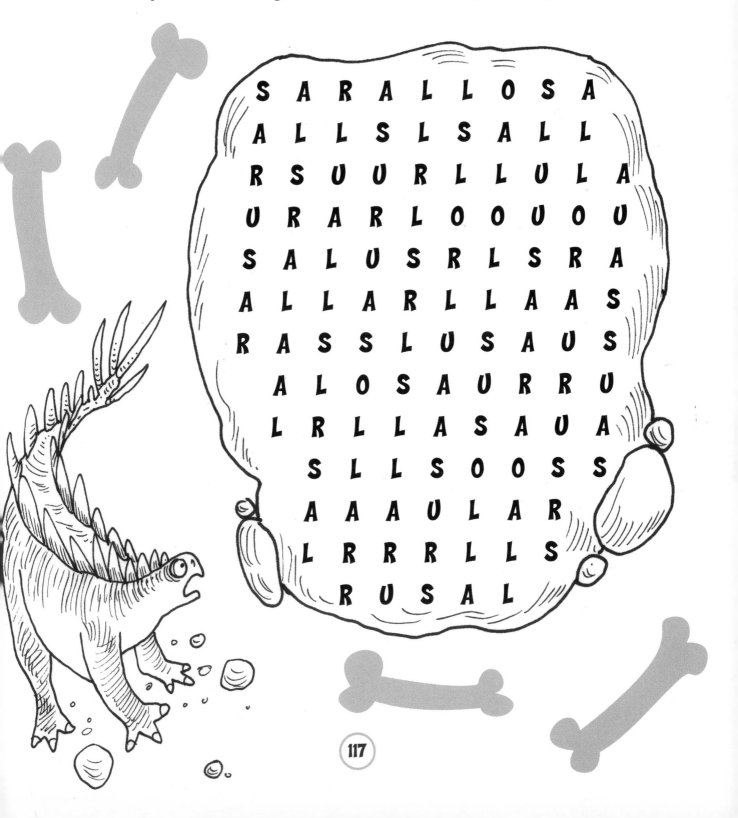

SHOE SECRETS

Tilly is tidying her shoes. She has named them
in code so that her sister can't borrow them!
What is in each box, if A = 6 and W = 2?

a

23.10.9
21.26.18.21.24

b

7.17.6.8.16
7.20.20.25.24

c

7.17.26.10
24.6.19.9.6.17.24

d

7.23.20.2.19
17.20.6.11.10.23.24

SPACE RACE

Study the skies to find ten differences between these two pictures.

FOLLOW THAT CAR

Spy HQ have contacted you with a licence plate that you must look out for. Which of these cars should you tail?

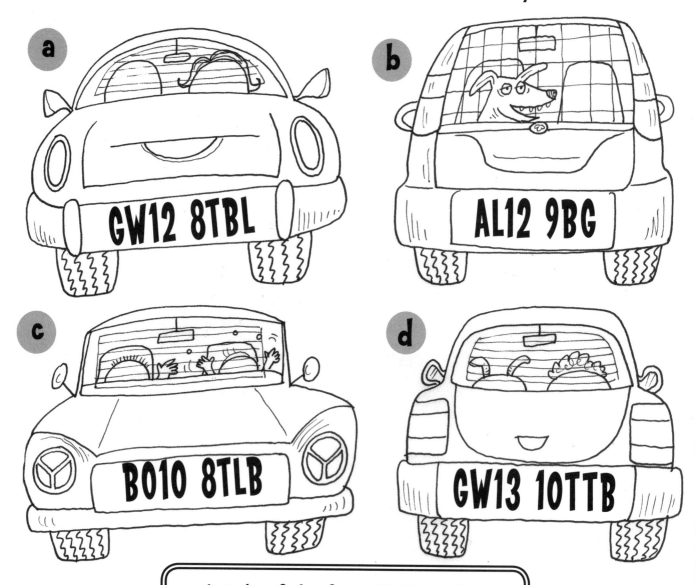

Initials of the first US President

Months in a year

Planets in our solar system

Initials of WWW inventor

SEEING THE SIGHTS

Work out which letters of the alphabet are missing each time to find the countries where you can see these sights.

BCOPWXFQRSU
VGDEKMNHJZ

AOVBCNWDKLFQ
RSUHXIJMZ

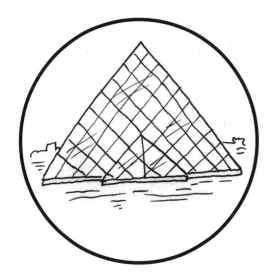

BOPQSMXTUH
IJKVLYWDGZ

WEIRD NATURE

Hmm, something's wrong here! Circle five peculiar things in this picture.

TREASURE TRAIL

Follow the arrows in the direction they are pointing to help Nigel the cabin boy find his way to the treasure.

BACKBONES

Which two sets of letters can be unscrambled to spell VERTEBRAE?

TEBERRVEE

VABERAERT

BERTERVERA

AREBEERVT

BARTEVEBE

BEADY EYED

Look really closely to find two of these necklaces
that match each other perfectly.

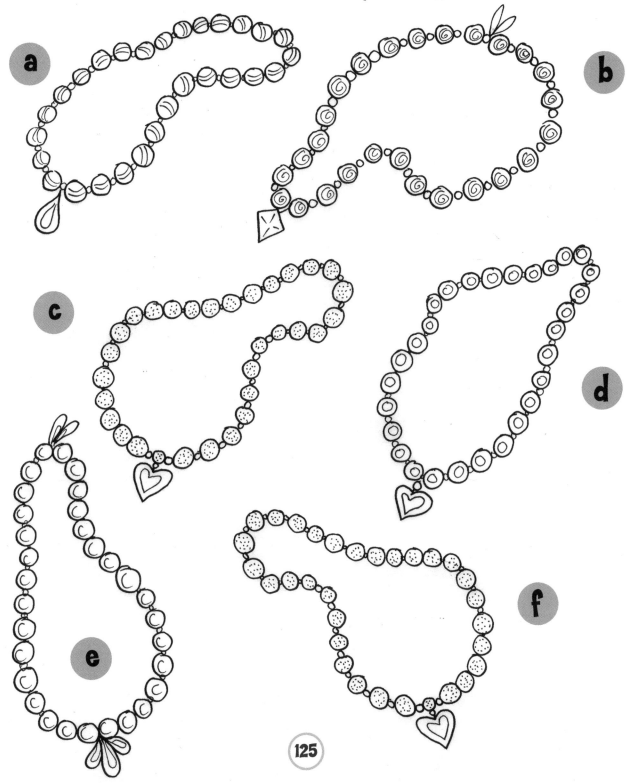

ALIEN LIFE

Do you believe aliens exist? What do you think they look like?

SQUARE EYES

Agent Neutrino has been locked up, and his captors will only let him out if he can solve this challenge. He needs your help!

Move only two coins to turn this triangle into a square.

ALL GONE

Which of the seven wonders were these tourists hoping to see?
Use the grid code to spell it out.

	1	2	3	4
a	R	A	L	T
b	N	U	D	O
c	E	C	F	P
d	S	B	Y	H

c2.b4.a3.b4.d1.d1.b2.d1

b4.c3

a1.d4.b4.b3.c1.d1

BEST IN SHOW

Study the pet show picture carefully and find each of the circled items.

SHIP'S COOK

The crew of this ship are hungry but the cook is running out of food. See if you can solve his problem.

1. He gives Pirate Mo half of the maggoty biscuits in his jar, plus half a biscuit.

2. He gives Pirate Po half of the remaining maggoty biscuits, plus half a biscuit.

3. He gives Pirate Jo half of what's left, plus half a biscuit. Now all the maggoty biscuits are gone.

How many maggoty biscuits were there in the jar to start with?

DINO DOODLE

Use the grid lines to help you copy this ankylosaurus.
Add some plants in the background if you like.

ALL THAT GLITTERS

How many words containing three or more letters can you make from the phrase below? One has been done to get you started.

DIAMONDS ARE FOREVER

1. DESIRE

2. _____

3. _____

4. _____

5. _____

6. _____

7. _____

8. _____

9. _____

10. _____

11. _____

12. _____

13. _____

14. _____

15. _____

16. _____

SPACE-DOKU

Fill in the grid so that each row, column, and minigrid contains each of the space symbols.

ON A MISSION

Use the clues to work out which spy is which, and where they will be posted on their next mission.

	JO	BO	MO
USA			
AUSTRALIA			
NEW ZEALAND			

Jo has very straight hair.

Mo is a man.

The female is going to the USA.

Jo is going to New Zealand.

	1	2	3
JO			
BO			
MO			

AMAZING!

Find a way through the maze to the fantastic
Statue of Liberty at the end.

RUFF OUTLINE

Only one of these shadows matches the main picture. Which one is it?

AROUND THE WORLD

Cross out every other letter, starting with O, to find three islands that Pirate Dan is planning to plunder.

HATCHLINGS

What's curled up inside this prehistoric egg?
Is it a tiny dinosaur, or a baby bird?

BALLET CLASS

Look carefully to find each of the music and ballet words hidden in the grid. They can be found across, up and down, and diagonally.

E	O	B	A	T	T	P	I	R	L	P	E
O	C	R	E	L	E	V	E	H	L	B	P
B	E	U	Q	S	E	B	A	R	A	A	P
P	A	A	E	U	B	P	R	P	B	T	A
R	E	L	T	P	E	A	L	E	T	T	E
B	C	L	T	O	P	I	L	E	L	E	R
E	A	E	E	I	E	T	T	L	O	M	C
P	T	L	U	N	B	A	R	R	O	E	O
P	B	E	O	T	L	E	G	V	T	N	U
A	A	L	R	E	O	E	R	E	E	T	P
H	T	E	I	P	L	B	A	L	N	Q	E
C	T	V	P	L	E	S	Q	U	D	U	E
E	E	E	A	B	A	R	R	E	U	E	R

ALLEGRO
ECHAPPE
PIROUETTE
BARRE
RELEVE
BATTEMENT

TENDU
PLIE
COUPE
ARABESQUE
POINTE
BALLON

LEARN THE LINGO

Use the code book to work out what these aliens are trying to tell us.

SPY SPOTTING

There are ten differences between these two pictures.
See if you're well-trained enough to spot them!

MEGA NUMBERS

The Ancient Greeks were pretty good mathematicians. See how you measure up: which three numbers here add up to exactly 100?

43

52

76

38

45

15

12

27

BABY TALK

Work out which letters of the alphabet are missing each time, and use them to spell three baby animals. Which of the animals shown does not have its baby here?

BHIJKR
STUDEGWXV
CMNPQYZ

CHIJDO
PWXYSTEFQ
RKNUVGZ

BSGHIQ
RTUVDKMNO
EWXJPYZ

BUMPY RIDE

There's a poor snail somewhere in this scene. Look carefully to spot it.

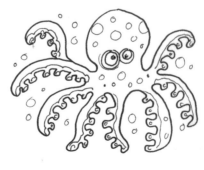

MATCHASAURUS

Each of the dinosaurs on this page has a twin - or have they?
Look carefully to see if any don't pair up.

TOP SHOP

Shopping can be such hard work! Which set of letters cannot be unscrambled to spell the word BOUTIQUE correctly?

QUITEBOU

TOBQUIUE

BUTOIQUE

QUIBOUTIE

EQUIUTBO

ALIEN ENCOUNTER

All of these aliens look odd to us - but which one is the odd one out?

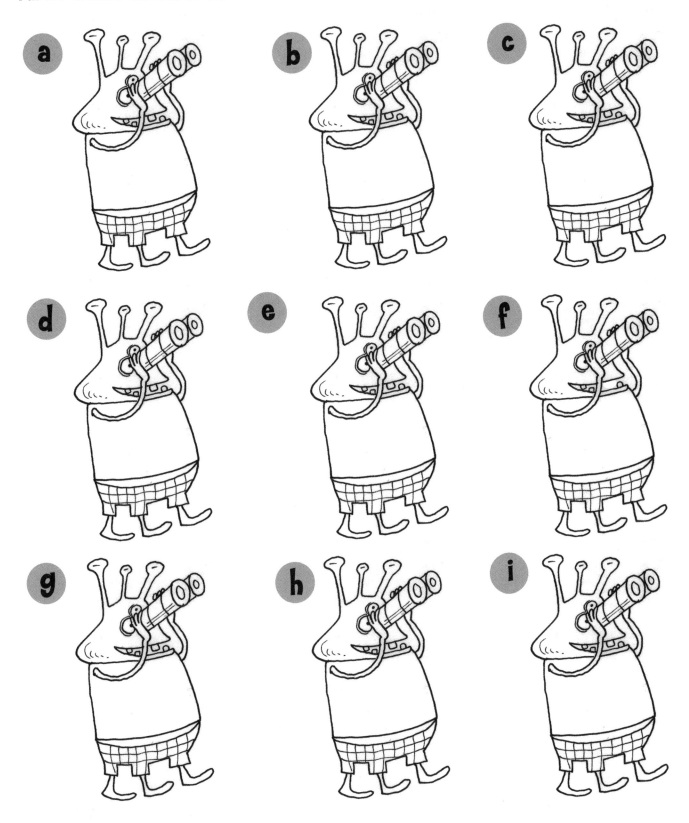

VILLAINOUS VINNIE

Meet Vinnie - an evil mastermind planning to take over the world with his wicked invention. But what mean machine has he made? Draw it here.

PYRAMID PUZZLE

Move three sticks to make four equal-sided triangles
- with no sticks overlapping.

TAKE A LONG LOOK

Look carefully to find the word GIRAFFE hidden just once in this grid.

G	i	R	F	E	A	R	G	i	R
i	f	i	G	i	R	A	E	E	G
R	G	F	A	i	R	G	F	G	E
F	i	E	G	i	R	F	G	i	R
E	R	F	R	A	A	E	i	R	A
G	A	R	F	R	G	A	R	F	G
A	F	E	i	G	i	G	A	A	i
R	F	G	i	R	R	i	R	i	R
A	G	i	R	E	F	F	E	R	A
G	R	i	F	R	G	G	F	i	E
E	A	F	R	G	R	i	i	E	F
i	G	i	R	A	F	R	A	R	E
E	R	E	F	i	E	R	F	G	A
G	i	R	E	F	F	E	R	F	i
F	E	A	G	i	R	A	F	i	G

ALL AT SEA

Can you find the circled items in the picture below.
Don't get caught in the crossfire!

BRAIN FOOD

How brainy are you feeling? Work out this mighty puzzle if you can!

If 6 dinosaurs munch 6 plants in 6 minutes, how many dinosaurs will it take to munch 60 plants in 60 minutes?

DRESS DESIGNER

Use the grids to help you copy these fashion outlines,
and then customize them with your own style.

A ROCKY RIDE

Watch out! We're entering the area between Mars and Jupiter. Use your wits to see how many words of three letters or more you can make out of the phrase below. One has been done to help you.

ASTEROID BELT

1. SOLID
2. _____
3. _____
4. _____
5. _____
6. _____
7. _____
8. _____
9. _____
10. _____
11. _____
12. _____
13. _____
14. _____
15. _____
16. _____

TOTALLY BRILLIANT
COOL
PUZZLE
BOOK

ANSWERS

3 DINOSAUR BONES
SPINOSAURUS

4 FORTY WINKS
e

5 PARADISE GARDENS

7 BLAST OFF

8 UNDER ORDERS
CATCH THE MIDNIGHT
TRAIN TO MILAN

9 AMAZON ADVENTURE

10   OLDER AND WISER

a

11   CAPTAIN'S CALL

TIME TO WORK, SCUM BAGS!

12   PREHISTORIC PUZZLER

13   EAR WE GO

Two are left over

14   WRITTEN IN THE STARS

GALAXY, PLANET, ASTRONAUT,
SHUTTLE, SUPERNOVA
Shuttle and planet have the
wrong labels.

15   SPY SKILLS

a and f

17   TURN AROUND

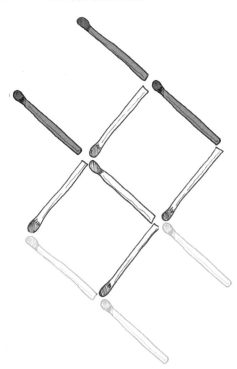

18   PRETTY POLLY

R	A	T	T	A	R	P	A	T
P	A	R	T	P	A	O	R	P
O	T	P	A	R	A	T	T	A
R	P	R	O	T	P	A	R	R
T	O	T	O	P	A	T	A	O
A	T	O	R	R	A	P	A	O
R	P	O	R	R	A	T	P	T
R	O	T	O	P	A	R	T	O
A	O	P	A	T	O	R	A	P

19 STEP BACK iN TiME

20 ACCE$$ORiE$
a = 17.50
b = 17.25
c = 17

22 TOP SECRET
Here are some you may have found: flour, ferry, fury, furry, rosy, soon, sorry, four, eyeful, felony

23 DREAM DESTiNATiON
Number 3 is missing

2	3	4	1	6	5
5	1	6	4	2	3
4	5	3	2	1	6
6	2	1	5	3	4
3	4	2	6	5	1
1	6	5	3	4	2

24 MAN'S BEST FRiEND
g

25 UNDER FiRE

26   LOOK OUT!
e

27   COVER UP
BLAZER

29   FOREIGN EXCHANGE

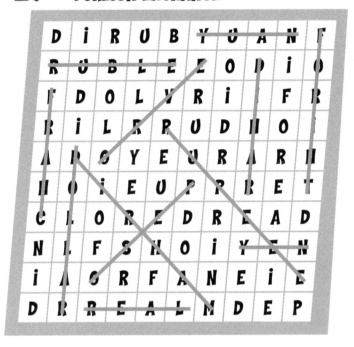

30   WHAT ON EARTH?
ONLY ONE OF THE SEVEN
WONDERS OF THE WORLD
REMAINS STANDING.

31   BIRDS OF A FEATHER

32   TREASURE TRAIL
The pirate on the left

33   READY FOR BATTLE
SPIKE

34   IT MUST BE GLOVE
15

35 SKY MAP

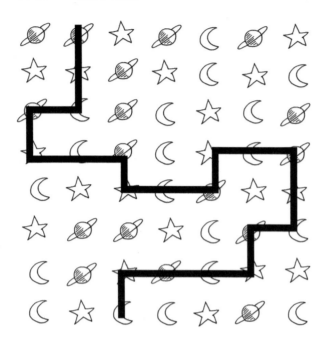

36 DECODED

CHERARWATBE

37 GOING STRAIGHT

f

39 DUPED!

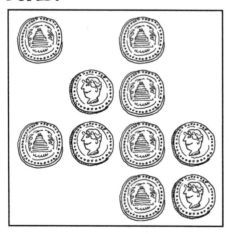

40 DEM BONES

6 times

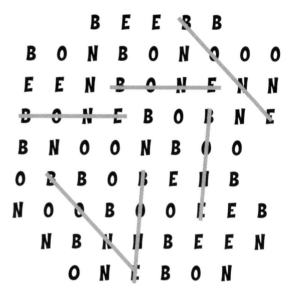

41 CATWALK CRAZY

160

42 BRAIN TEST

Switches c and f so you get:
$27 + 15 + 6 + 18 + 22 + 12 = 100$

44 ANCIENT WONDER

Here are some you may have found: hinge, inner, gears, diner, earns, air, design, head, hands, drainage

45 MOO-DOKU

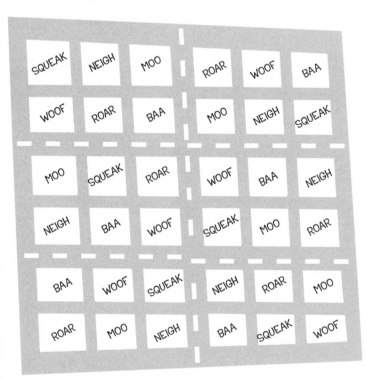

46 SAILING THE SEAS

Peter is going to Jamaica and owns a cat.
Julian is going to Puerto Rico and owns a parrot.
Jake is going to China and owns a snake.

47 FANCY FLIER

Exit b

48 MYSTERY MANNEQUIN

f

49 FAR FLUNG
VENUS

51 TOP OF THE WORLD

52 ZOO TRIP
The signs say TOILET, CAFE, FARM.
Here's the whole code filled in:

L	◗	V	▢	C	✳	O	❙	U	✳	B	★	X	✴	'	☆
?	✳	Q	✳	K	✚	!	✺	H	✤	"	✪	P	✴	E	◖
G	❖	D	▼	Y	●	A	▲	T	◆	N	☆	W	✛	i	✳
O	✳	S	◆	F	✵	M	■	J	✧	R	★	Z	✳	;	✡

53 READY, AIM, FIRE!

54 OLDER THAN OLD
Bagaceratops (at the bottom)
lived most recently.
Coelophysis (at the top) lived the
longest time ago.
These are the answers:
$50 \times 6 + 40 - 20 \div 8 = 40$
$14 + 33 \times 2 + 100 - 19 \div 5 = 35$
$212 - 80 \div 6 - 7 \times 2 = 30$

55 DRESSING UP
BELT, CROWN

56 WATERY WORLD
10

57 POINTING THE FINGER
Painting = c
Crown = d
Trophy = b
Phone = a

58 A LITTLE BIT LOST
AIDIN = INDIA which is in Asia
LAURITASA = AUSTRALIA which is in Australasia
CRANEF = FRANCE which is in Europe
NEAKY = KENYA which is in Africa
NACAAD = MEXICO which is in North America
LAIRBZ = BRAZIL which is in South America

59 PROUD AS A PEACOCK
e and i

61 TROODON AND THE TWIGS

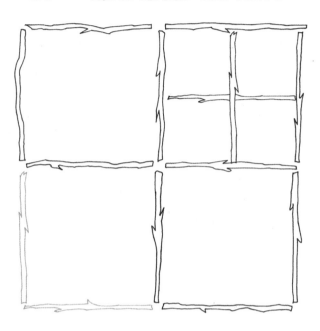

62 GIRL'S BEST FRIENDS

63 GALACTIC GOODIES

64 HOUSE ARREST

House number 23 is correct.

66 HOP IT!

Here are some you may have found: unit, urban, aunt, burnt, barn, train, tuna, air, bait, brain

67 TROPICAL TIME

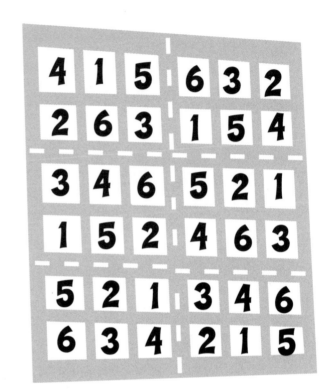

68 EGGS-ACTLY

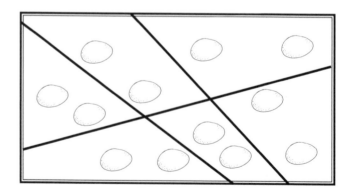

69 SHOPPING TRIP

73 FEATHERED FRIENDS

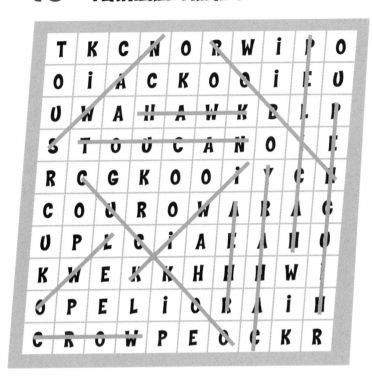

70 3-2-1-LIFTOFF

C

71 MAKE HASTE!

FOLLOW THE MAN IN THE VAN

74 SAY WHAT?

WELL CURSE MY CUTLASS
AND KNOCK ME DOWN
WITH A PARROT FEATHER!

75 NIGHT AT THE MUSEUM

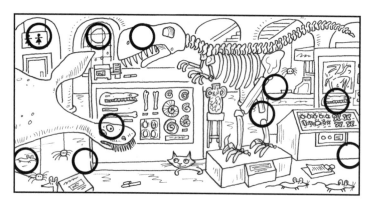

76 SAFE STASH
9583

77 SPACE-TIME
WORK, MEAL, REST, CALL HOME

78 SHALL WE DANCE?
10

79 HIT THE RIGHT NOTES

80 GOING APE
ANGUTORAN

81 ODDER AND ODDER
f

83 HATS OFF!
She owns 9 white hats.

84 SEEING STARS
1. COMET
2. ASTEROID
3. RED GIANT
4. NEBULA

85 SOMETHING SUSPICIOUS

86 TRAVEL GUIDE

a = 99
b = 85
c = 120
d = 135

88 WAKEY WAKEY!

Here are some you may have found: serve, mist, merit, birth, mister, rest, rise, sherbet, severe, member

89 DINO-DOKU

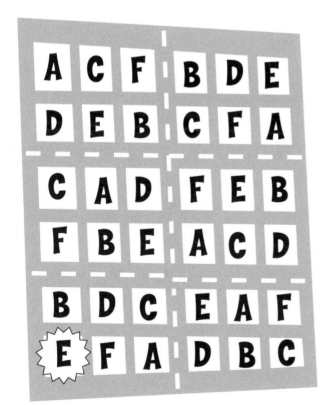

90 DESIGN DIVA

b

91 SUPERNOVA

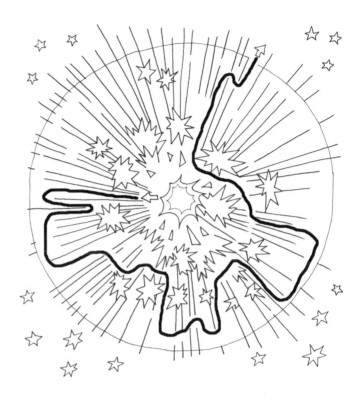

92 MRS BAD GUY

e

93 TAKE ME TO THE TEMPLE

TURKEY

95 ROLL CALL

Palmer, Perry and Presley are missing.

96 DINO CODE

Styracosaurus, Minmi

97 WEDDING BELLES

98 LET ME IN!

612814

99 ON THE RUN

PRAGUE

100 MISSING THE POINT

101 CHANGING TIMES

d

102 ALL AT SEA

UCCANNEBR

103 DUCK-BILLS

e

168

105 SPACE DOG

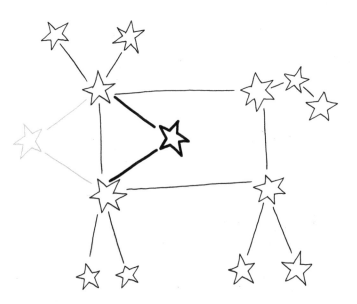

107 WONDERS OF THE SEA

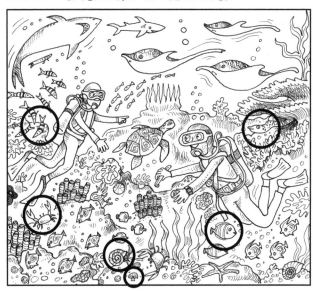

108 PET PRESENTS

A bone on its own costs 2.50.

110 RUN AWAY!

Here are some you may have found: aunt, roast, noun, arrest, annoys, nose, oyster, nurse, earns, nature

106 DOUBLE AGENT

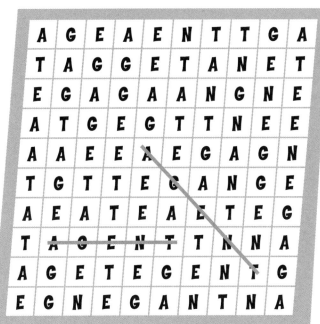

111   GEM-DOKU

113   HUNT HIM DOWN

112   ALIEN WORKOUT

Piff is number 1 and is from the planet Jootle.

Burp is number 2 and is from the planet Snark.

Paff is number 3 and is from the planet Bilge.

114   AMAZING ATOMIUM

d

115   ON THE MOVE

MOLLUSC

117 ALL FOR ONE

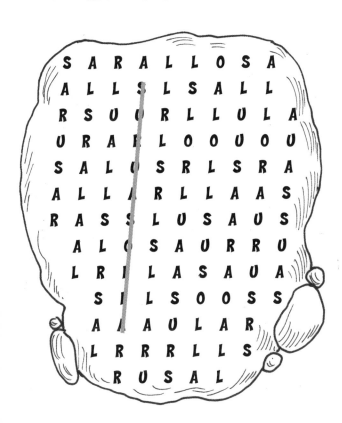

118 SHOE SECRETS
a = RED PUMPS
b = BLACK BOOTS
c = BLUE SANDALS
d = BROWN LOAFERS

119 SPACE RACE

120 FOLLOW THAT CAR
a. GW12 8TBL
Initials of the first US President
= GW (George Washington)
Months in a year = 12
Planets in our solar system = 8
Initials of WWW inventor = TBL
(Tim Berners Lee)

121 SEEING THE SIGHTS
ITALY
EGYPT
FRANCE

122 WEIRD NATURE

123 TREASURE TRAIL

124 BACKBONES
VABERAERT
AREBEERVT

125 BEADY EYED
c and f

127 SQUARE EYES

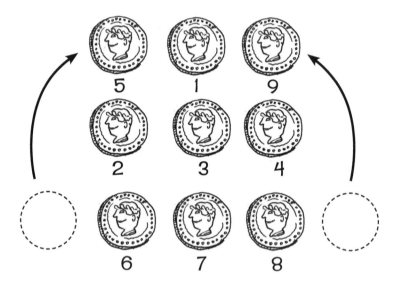

128 ALL GONE
COLOSSUS OF RHODES

129 BEST IN SHOW

130 SHIP'S COOK

There were 7 maggoty biscuits there in the jar to start with. He gave Pirate Mo half of the biscuits, plus half a biscuit = $3\frac{1}{2} + \frac{1}{2}$ (leaving 3 biscuits) He gave Pirate Po half of the remaining biscuits, plus half a biscuit = $1\frac{1}{2} + \frac{1}{2}$ (leaving 1 biscuit) He gives Pirate Jo half of what was left, plus half a biscuit = $\frac{1}{2} + \frac{1}{2}$

132 ALL THAT GLITTERS

Here are some you may have found: reins, river, nose, ransom, fame, ends, rose, drama, ease, modern

133 SPACE-DOKU

134 ON A MISSION

1 is Bo and she's going to the USA.
2 is Jo and he's going to New Zealand.
3 is Mo and he's going to Australia.

135 AMAZING!

136 RUFF OUTLINE

f

137 AROUND THE WORLD

CUBA
JAMAICA
BAHAMAS

139 BALLET CLASS

E O B A T T P I R L P E
O C R E L E V E H L B P
B E U Q S E B A R A A P
P A A E U R P R B B T A
R E L T P E A L E T T E
B C L T O P T E L E R
A E E I Z T T O N C
P T L O N B A R R E O
P B E O T L E G V T O
A A L B E O R E E T P
N T E T P L B A N Q E
C T V P L E S Q U U E
E E E A B A R R E U E R

140 LEARN THE LINGO

DON'T FORGET YOUR SUNSCREEN

141 SPY SPOTTING

144 BUMPY RIDE

142 MEGA NUMBERS

43 + 12 + 45 = 100

143 BABY TALK

The baby animals are foal, lamb, calf. The cat and dog do not have their babies here.

145 MATCHASAURUS

146   TOP SHOP
QUIBOUTIE

147   ALIEN ENCOUNTER
f

149   PYRAMID PUZZLE

150   TAKE A LONG LOOK

151   READY, AIM, FIRE!

152   BRAIN FOOD

6 dinosaurs. Here's why:
6 dinosaurs munch 6 plants in
6 minutes. Multiply by ten, to get
60 plants and 60 minutes, and
you still need 6 dinosaurs.

154   A ROCKY RIDE

Here are some you may have
found: sort, rest, riot, store,
rose, tile, list, stir, slide, able